On behalf of CAP.INSTITUTO

In the realm of letters, where words intertwine, CAP Institute extends gratitude, truly divine. To seekers of puzzles, to minds that explore, Your passion for words, we deeply adore.

In each hidden grid, a challenge embraced, With diligence and joy, your time you've traced. For every seeker, every curious mind, Thank you for the journey, so beautifully designed.

This Book Belongs to:

____

Welcome to "MindMaze Challenges - Crosswords and Labyrinths," CAP.INSTITUTE's latest creation for ages 7 to 45. Dive into a world where words and mazes merge, providing a stimulating intellectual experience.

Professionalism and innovation shine in crafted challenges, enhancing critical thinking. From enriching crosswords to mind-bending labyrinths, "MindMaze Challenges" is our commitment to cognitive development through engaging puzzles.

Within these pages, a symphony of linguistic and spatial challenges awaits, offering an indispensable companion for learners and thinkers alike. Elevate your cognitive prowess, unlocking new realms of knowledge. Acquire your copy today, embarking on a journey where every word and twist reveals the key to a captivating world of intellect and fun.

CAP.INSTITUTE©

Crossword - Level 1

2.Tall, rocky elevation with snow on top.   1.Entertaining problem-solving activity with pieces.

Labyrinth - level 1

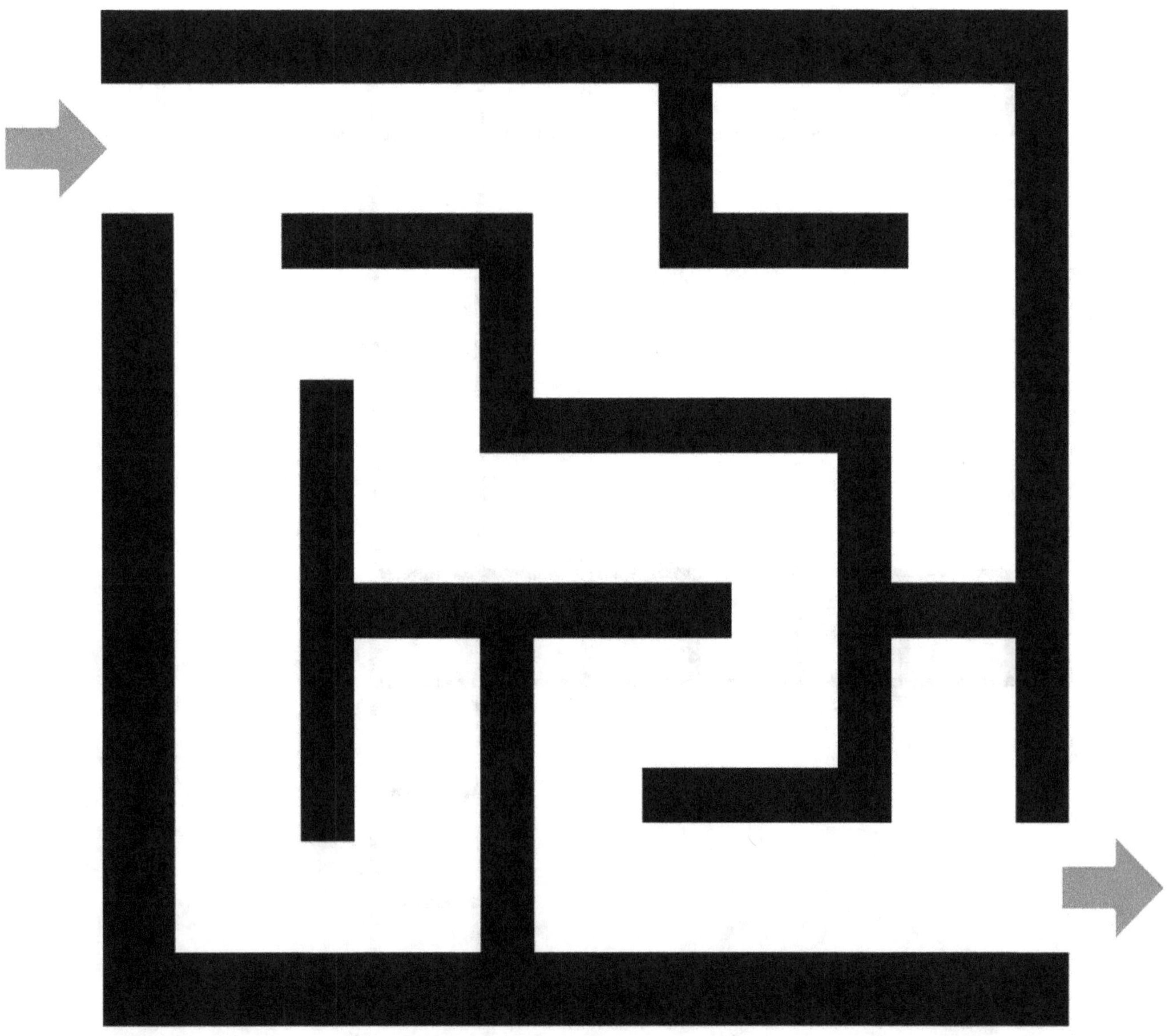

Crossword - Level 2

1.Giant mammal

3.Musical instrument

2.Space traveler

Labyrinth - level 2

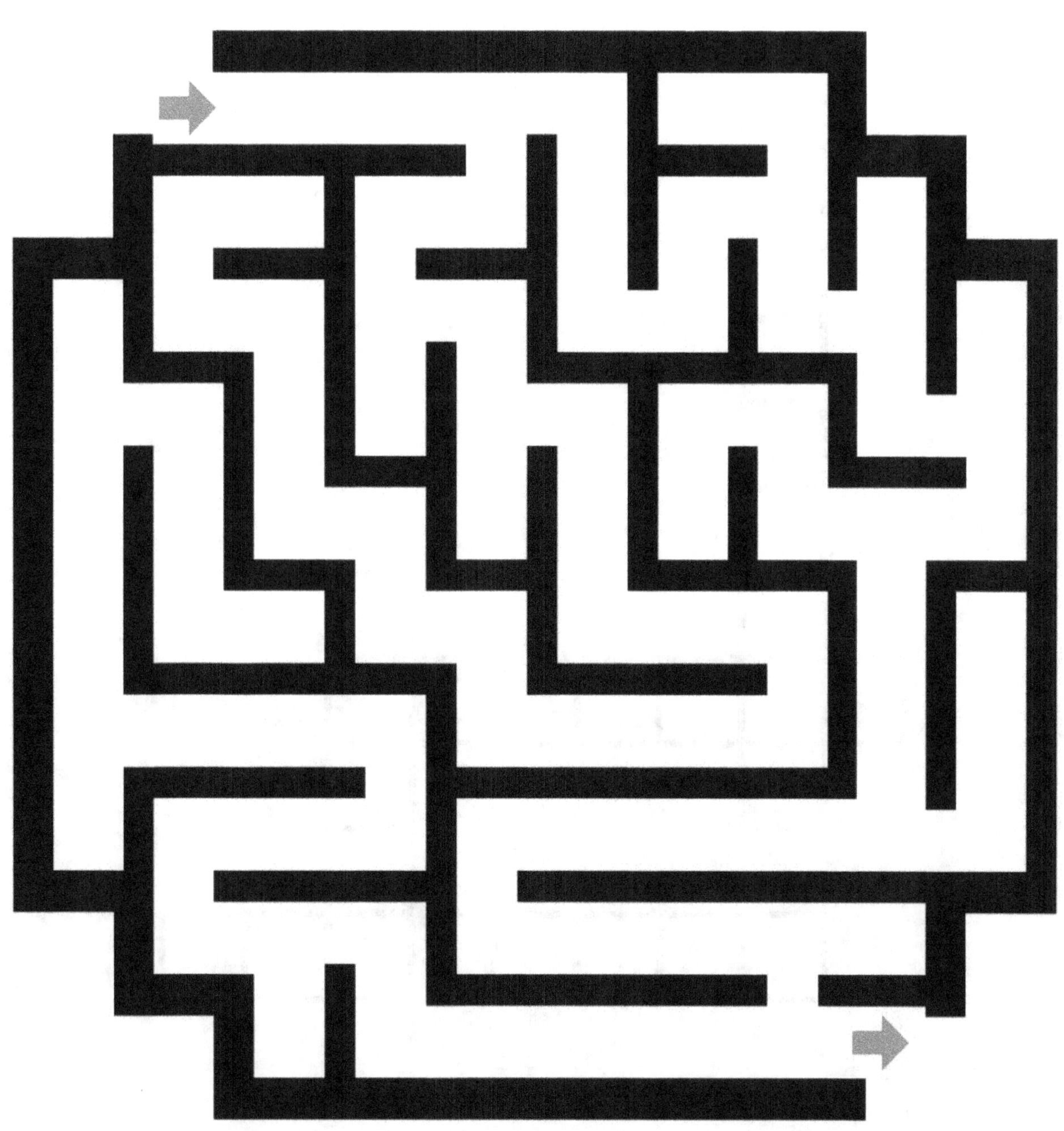

Crossword - Level 3

3.Waterfall descent.
4.Idealistic but impractical.

1.Fleeting and transient.
2.Highest point or peak.

Labyrinth - level 3

Crossword - Level 4

3.A bright yellow bloom.
4.A series of small waterfalls.
5.Speaking in a soft, hushed tone.

1.Something unknown or puzzling.
2.A vast system of stars and cosmic matter.

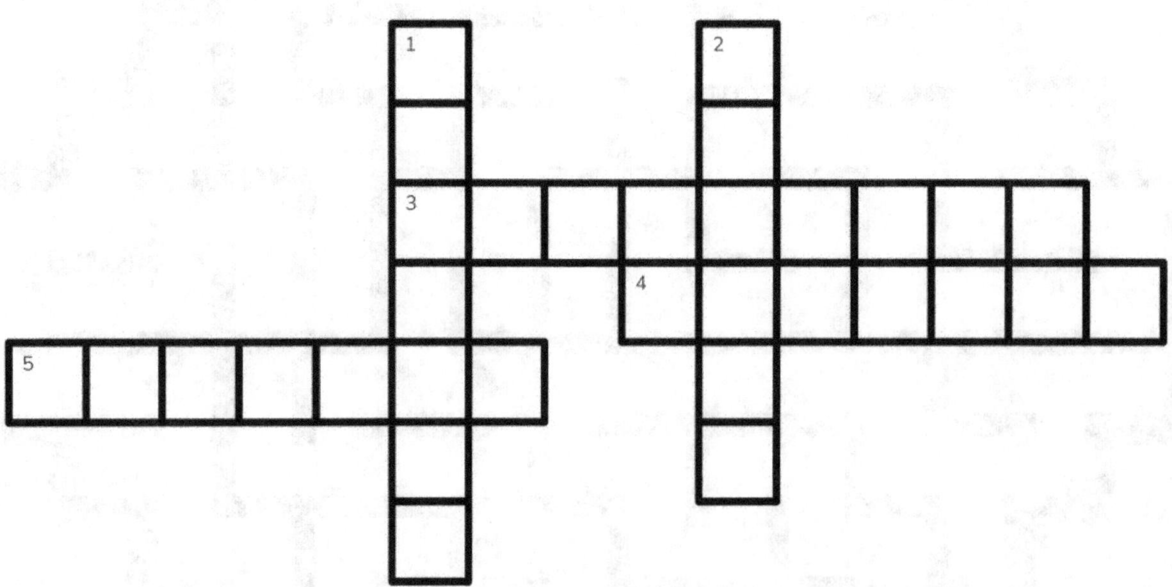

Labyrinth - level 4

Crossword - Level 5

3.Travel aimlessly or without a plan.
4.Something unexplained or unknown.
5.Puzzling or mysterious situation.
6.Source of warmth and light.

1.State of peaceful coexistence.
2.Musical performance expressing love.

Labyrinth - level 5

Crossword - Level 6

3.Home where eggs are carefully laid.
4.Their sweet vocalization in nature.
6.Common food source for many.

1.Feathers allow them to fly.
2.Resting spot for tweeting creatures.
5.Colorful and distinctive bird feathers.

Labyrinth - level 6

Crossword - Level 7

2.A place where one resides permanently.
4.Natural environment for a specific organism.
6.A person's home or place of living.

1.A family's home and surrounding land.
3.Provides protection and a safe haven.
5.Where you spend your daily life.
7.A place of residence or habitation.

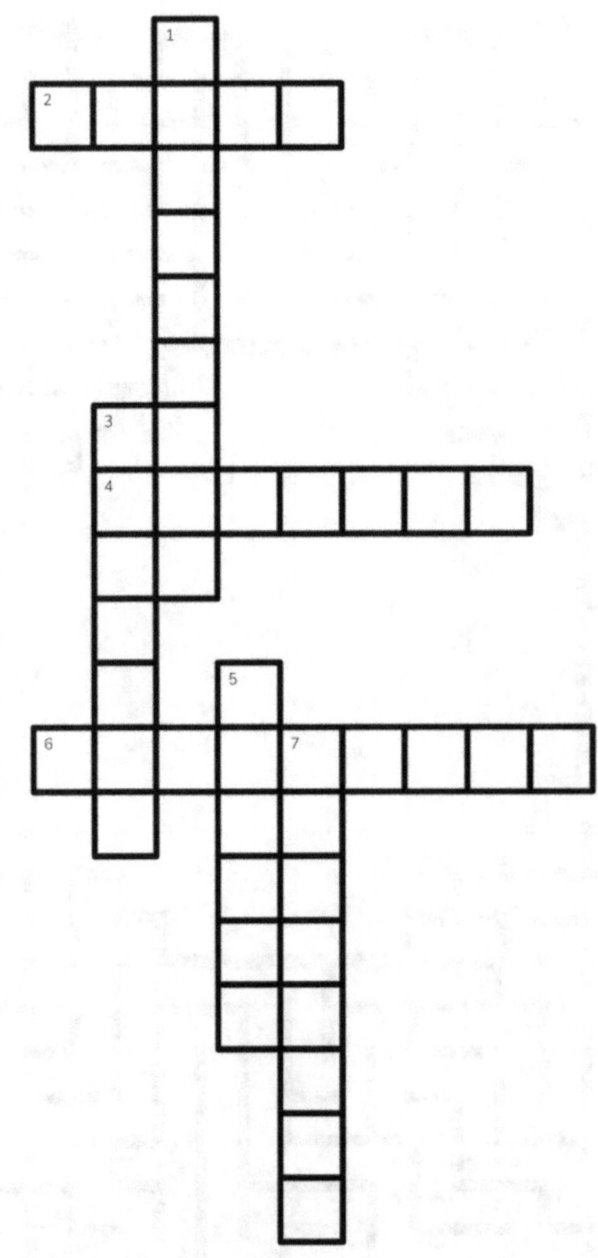

Labyrinth - level 7

Crossword - Level 8

2.Common countertop material
4.Sedimentary rock formed from marine organisms
5.Metamorphic rock used for roofing
6.Transparent mineral with geometrically arranged atoms
7.Engineered stone used in construction

1.Small, rounded stone found in rivers
3.Dark volcanic rock often used decoratively

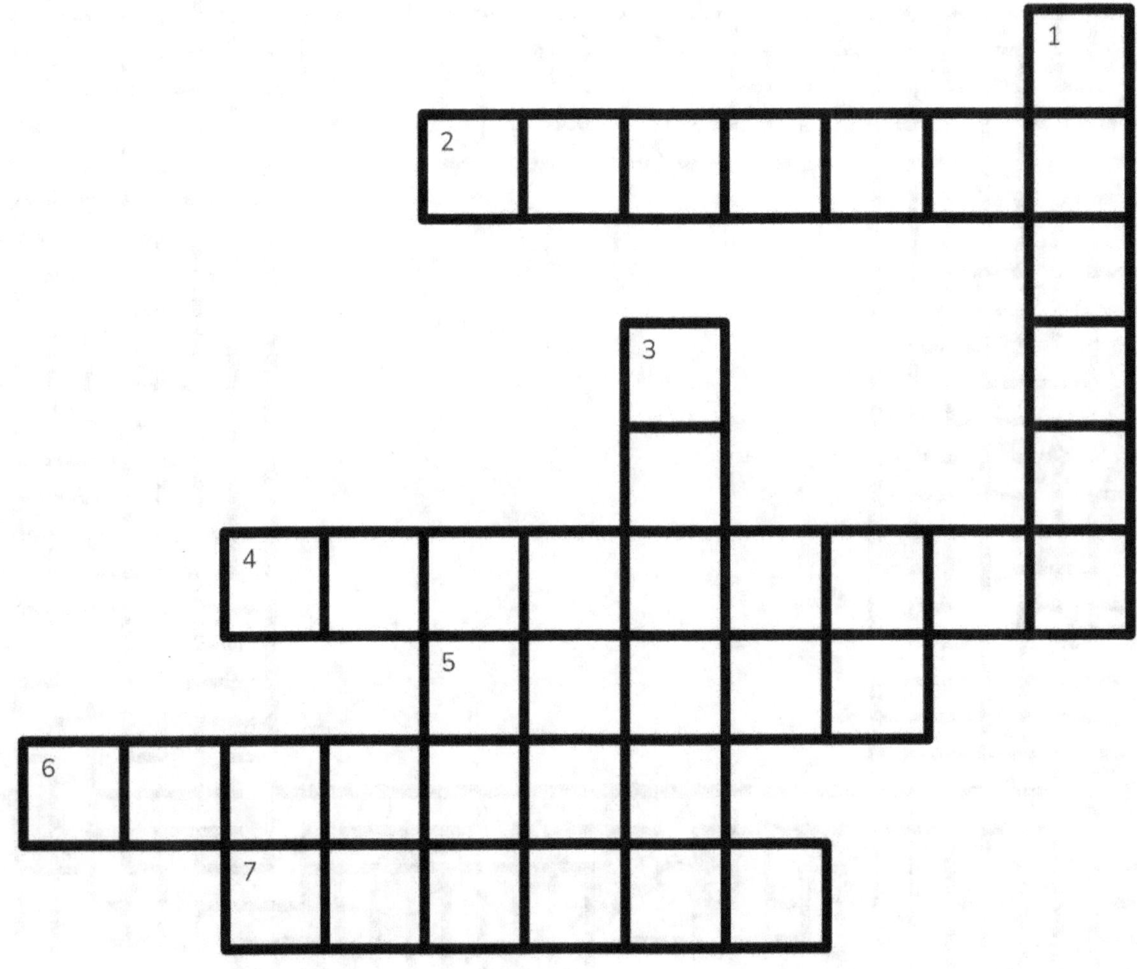

Labyrinth - level 8

Crossword - Level 9

3.Overflowing of water onto adjacent land.
5.A winding curve or bend in a river.
6.A smaller river that flows into a larger one.
7.A landform where a river meets a sea.
8.The wide mouth of a river at sea.

1.The point where two rivers meet.
2.The starting point of a river.
4.Fast-flowing, turbulent sections of a river.

Labyrinth - level 9

Crossword - Level 10

1. Organs for extracting oxygen from water.
4. Seasonal movement of fish for breeding or feeding.
7. Primary mode of locomotion for most fish.
8. Clownfish, known for living in sea anemones.

2. Bony plates covering a fish's skin.
3. Carnivorous fish found in South American rivers.
5. Used for propulsion and steering in water.
6. Shape that helps reduce water resistance.

Labyrinth - level 10

Crossword - Level 11

2.A symbol indicating the pitch of written musical notes.
3.The catchy part that repeats in a song.
4.The speed or pace of a musical piece.
6.A transitional section connecting different parts of a song.
9.The combination of different musical notes played together.

1.A section of a song with its own lyrics.
5.The main, memorable tune in a composition.
7.The pattern of beats in a musical piece.
8.A specific category or style of music.

Labyrinth - level 11

Crossword - Level 12

2.A symbol indicating the pitch of written musical notes.
3.The catchy part that repeats in a song.
4.The speed or pace of a musical piece.
6.A transitional section connecting different parts of a song.
9.The combination of different musical notes played together.

1.A section of a song with its own lyrics.
5.The main, memorable tune in a composition.
7.The pattern of beats in a musical piece.
8.A specific category or style of music.

Labyrinth - level 12

Crossword - Level 13

2.Destructive influence.
3.Fleeting moment.
5.Beyond description.
7.Aesthetic attractiveness.
8.Pleasant surprise.
9.Cryptography technique.
10.Describing a voice or melody.

1.Innate preference.
4.Insightful observation.
6.Pursuing impossible dreams.
8.Loquacious and verbose.

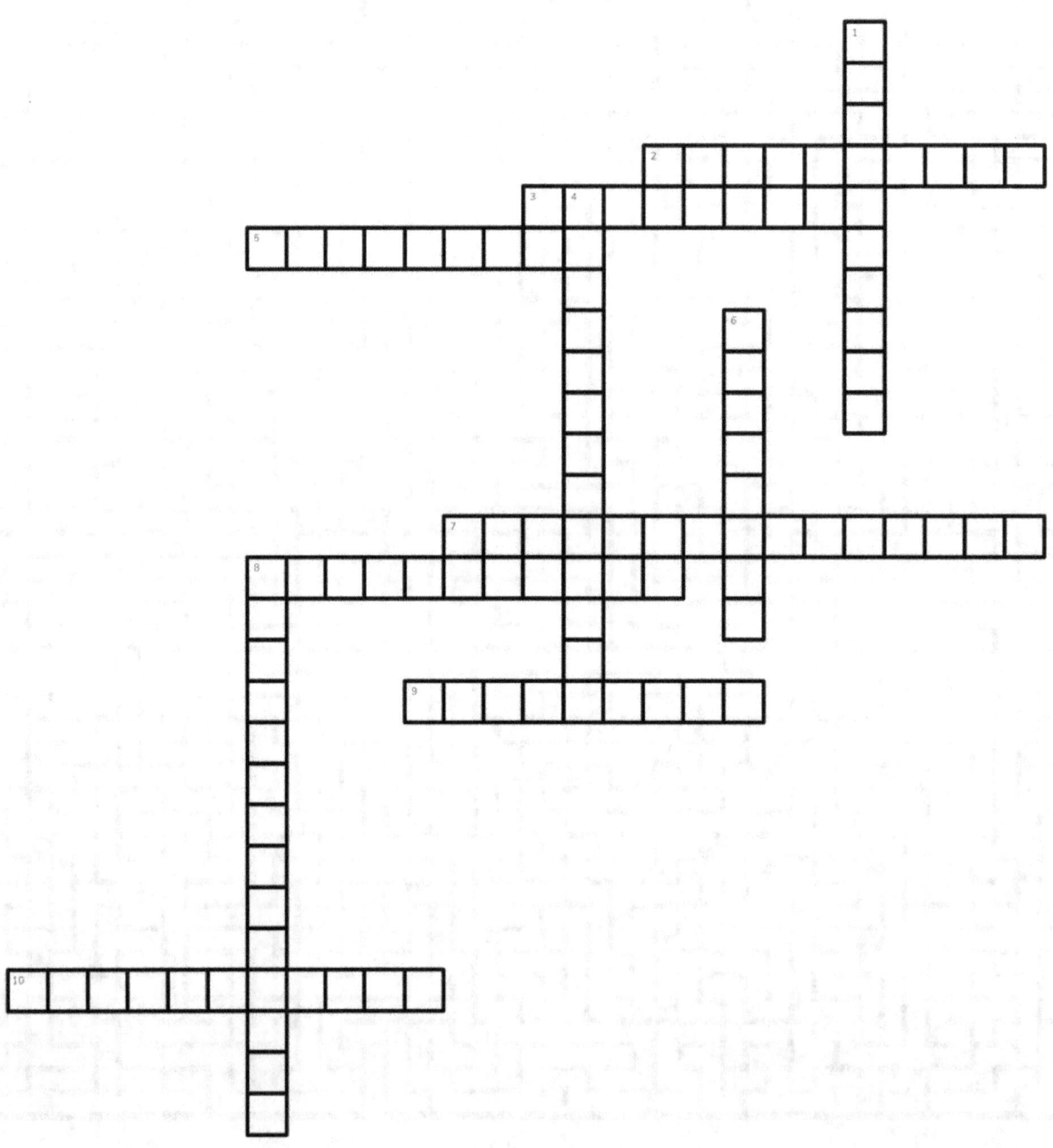

Labyrinth - level 13

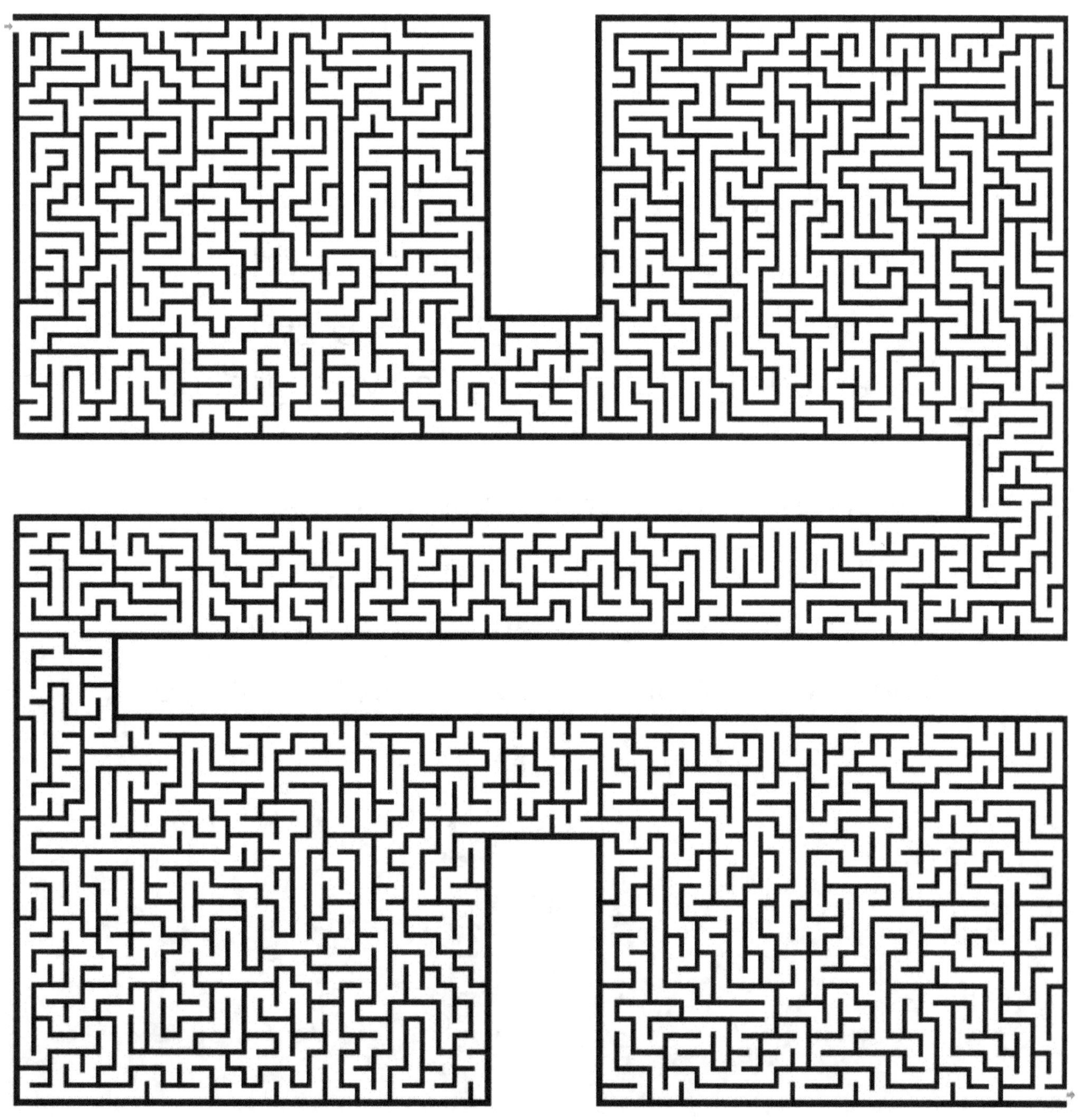

In the realm of words and winding paths,
CAP.INSTITUTE applauds the art of your journey.
Crossword challenges, unrevealed labyrinths,
A testament to your intellect, brave and bold.

Through enigmatic chapters, twists unfolded,
You embraced the puzzles that swirled.
With pens poised, minds engaged,
Gratitude for the curiosity you've engaged.

In this literary adventure, unique and entwined,
Our thanks for making it part of your fun.
To unsolved clues and paths untrod,
You're the explorer, and we're grateful, oh so.

100% ☐

50% ☐

1% ☐

CAP.INSTITUTE©

www.ingramcontent.com/pod-product-compliance
Lightning Source LLC
Chambersburg PA
CBHW080734260726
48660CB00010B/3843